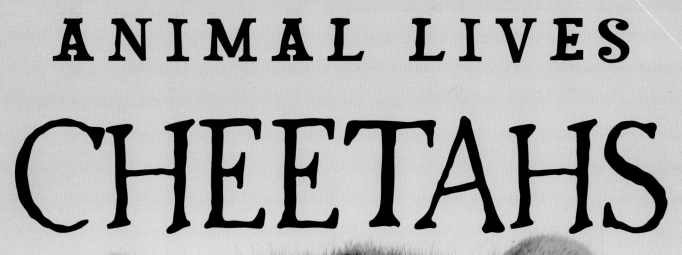

ANIMAL LIVES
CHEETAHS

Sally Morgan

QEB

QEB Publishing

Copyright © QEB Publishing 2014

Designed and edited by Calcium

First published in the United States in 2014 by
QEB Publishing, Inc.
3 Wrigley, Suite A
Irvine, CA 92618

www.qed-publishing.co.uk

A CIP record for this book is available from the Library of Congress.

ISBN: 978 1 78171 614 4

Printed in China

Photo credits
(t=top, b=bottom, l=left, r=right, c=centre, fc=front cover)

FLPA 1 Frans Lanting, 4–5 Stephen Belcher/Minden Pictures, 6–7 Frans Lanting, 7t Terry Whittaker, 7b Alain
Dragesco-Joffe/Biosphoto, 8–9 Tui De Roy/Minden Pictures, 10–11 Suzi Eszterhas/Minden Pictures, 11t Suzi
Eszterhas/Minden Pictures, 12–13 Suzi Eszterhas/Minden Pictures, 13t Bernd Rohrschneider, 14–15 Richard
Du Toit/Minden Pictures, 15t Christian Heinrich/Imagebroker, 16–17 Peter Davey, 17t Norbert Wu/Minden
Pictures, 18-19 Winfried Wisniewski/FN/Minden Pictures, 20 Frank Stober/Imagebroker, 22-23 Bernd Zoller/
Imagebroker, 23t Imagebroker, 25t Philip Perry, 25b Suzi Eszterhas/Minden Pictures, 27t Christiana Carvalho,
28-29 Imagebroker, 29t Malcolm Schuyl, 30l Ariadne Van Zandbergen, 31 Frans Lanting; **Getty Images** fc Suzi
Eszterhas/Minden Pictures; **Shutterstock** 2–3 Erwin Niemand, 5t Stayer, 15b Stu Porter, 19t LeonP,
20-21 Johannes Dag Mayer, 24-25 Stu Porter, 26-27
Juli Scalzi, 30t Achim Baque, 30br Gerry van der
Walt, 32 Johannes Dag Mayer, bc(l) Eric
Isselee, bc(r) Eric Isselee.

Contents

The cheetah

The cheetah is the fastest land animal in the world. It is a slim, long-legged big cat with a spotted coat. The cheetah is a type of mammal. Mammals are animals that have hair on their body and give birth to live young. Female mammals also produce milk for their babies.

FANTASTIC FACT

An adult cheetah weighs up to 138 pounds (63 kilograms). Its body can grow up to 5 feet (1.5 meters) long.

In the family

The cheetah's closest relatives are the other big cats, including the tiger (right), lion, and leopard.

A cheetah's long legs allow it to bound across the ground at great speed.

Predators!

Cheetahs are called **predators** because they hunt and eat other animals. A cheetah's prey includes deer, gazelles, and wildebeest.

Cheetah types

Most cheetahs have a golden-yellow coat that is covered with black spots. There is only one species, or type, of cheetah. However, there are small differences between cheetahs living in different parts of the world. Because of these differences, cheetahs are grouped into **subspecies**. There are three subspecies in Africa and two in Asia.

Cheetahs have two black stripes that run from the inside corner of their eyes to their mouth. These are called tear stripes.

FANTASTIC FACTS

The word "cheetah" comes from the Hindu word "chita," which means the "spotted one."

. . . .

The Asiatic cheetah's coat is perfectly colored for the grassland in which it lives.

King cheetah

The king cheetah from Africa (right) is a rare type of cheetah that has large black blotches rather than spots on its coat. Fewer than 50 king cheetahs have been seen in the wild. Most king cheetahs alive today have been bred in zoos and nature parks.

Desert cheetah

The Northwest African cheetah of the Sahara Desert has a much paler coat than most other cheetahs. The color of its coat helps it blend in with desert sand.

Where cheetahs live

Cheetahs were once found across all of Africa and the Middle East and as far east as India. Today, most cheetahs live in Africa, to the south of the Sahara Desert. Fewer than 100 cheetahs now live in Iran, in the Middle East. In recent years, only a few cheetahs have been seen in Pakistan.

Cheetahs like to live in open grassland, where they have plenty of space to run and hunt.

On the map

The areas in pink on this map show the parts of Africa and Asia where cheetahs live.

Africa

Asia

Indian Ocean

Cheetah habitats

Most cheetahs live on the African **savannah**. This is a huge, flat grassland with only a few trees—the perfect **habitat** for cheetahs. A few cheetahs also live on very dry grasslands near deserts or in colder mountainous areas.

FANTASTIC FACT

Most cheetahs are found in eastern and southwestern Africa. Many African cheetahs live in Namibia.

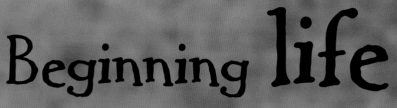

Beginning life

Once a female cheetah has mated with a male cheetah, she will be **pregnant** for about three months before giving birth to her **litter** of cubs. When they are born, cheetah cubs are helpless and cannot walk.

FANTASTIC FACTS

Most female cheetahs give birth to a litter of between three and five cubs. Sometimes, females have as many as eight cubs.
. . . .
Cheetah cubs are born with their eyes closed.

After birth, cheetah cubs start to feed on their mother's milk immediately.

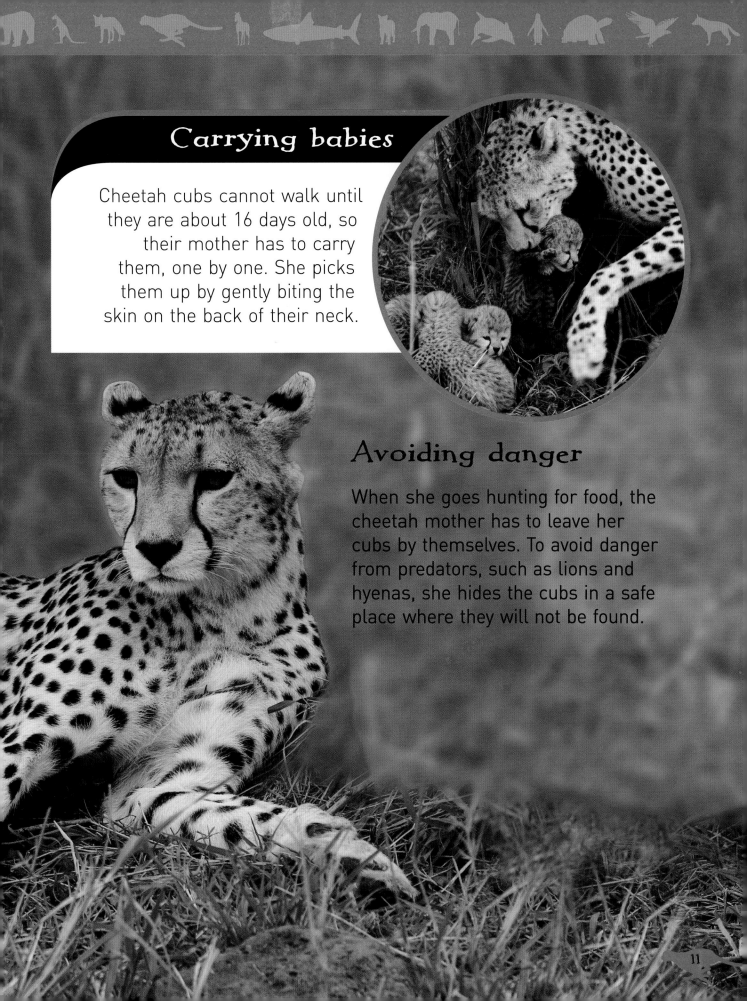

Carrying babies

Cheetah cubs cannot walk until they are about 16 days old, so their mother has to carry them, one by one. She picks them up by gently biting the skin on the back of their neck.

Avoiding danger

When she goes hunting for food, the cheetah mother has to leave her cubs by themselves. To avoid danger from predators, such as lions and hyenas, she hides the cubs in a safe place where they will not be found.

Growing up

For the first 12 weeks after they are born, the cheetah mother feeds the cubs her own milk. The cubs' first teeth begin to appear when they are three weeks old. By the time they are six weeks old, the cubs are able to follow their mother, and they begin to eat meat.

Playing helps cheetah cubs practice their hunting and fighting skills.

Learning to hunt

When the cubs are about seven months old, they join their mother on hunting trips. The cubs watch her hunt and quickly learn how to chase and catch their **prey**.

Cheetah family

The mother leaves her cubs when they are 14 to 18 months old. The female cubs stay in roughly the same area, but the males move faraway. The brothers in a litter stay together, sometimes for the rest of their lives.

FANTASTIC FACT

Only about one cheetah cub in every ten survives to three months old. Some cubs are killed by lions and hyenas and others die from disease and lack of food.

Cheetah movement

Although an adult cheetah can reach an amazing top speed of about 60 miles per hour (96 kilometers per hour) when it needs to, it usually runs at a slower 35 to 40 miles per hour (56 to 64 kilometers per hour) when chasing prey.

The cheetah gets very hot when running fast, so it can only run at top speed for about one minute.

Built for speed

The cheetah's slim body, long legs, and flexible back are built for speed. A cheetah can take long strides and move across the ground quickly. Large lungs allow it to breathe plenty of air.

FANTASTIC FACT

A cheetah can run 330 feet (100 meters) in less than four seconds. That is more than twice as fast as any human.

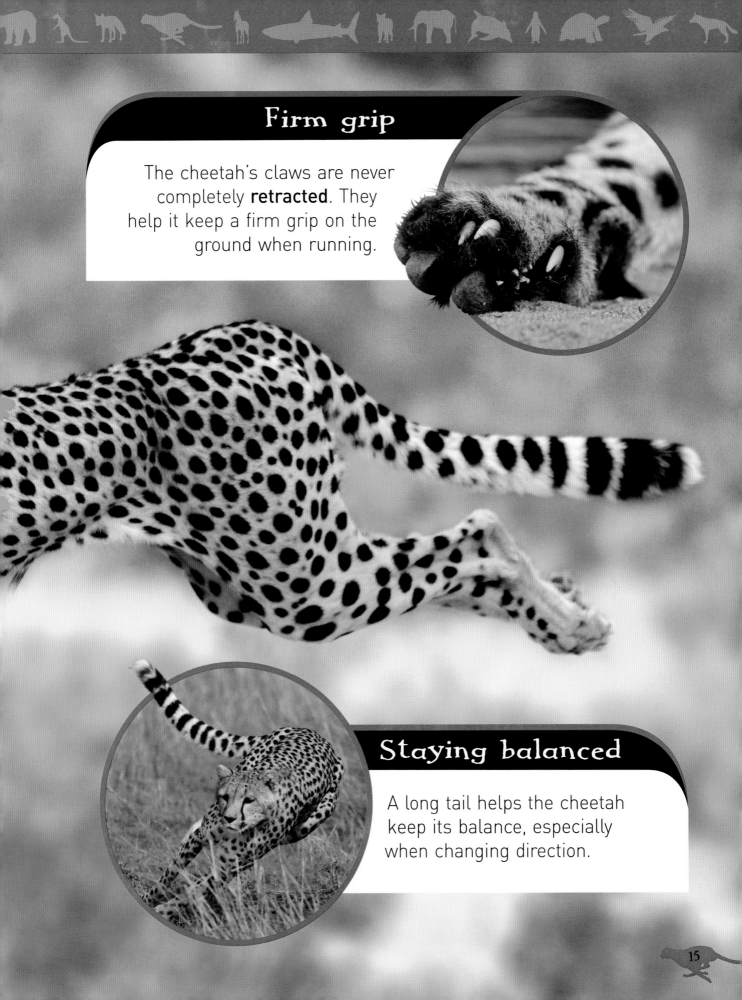

Firm grip

The cheetah's claws are never completely **retracted**. They help it keep a firm grip on the ground when running.

Staying balanced

A long tail helps the cheetah keep its balance, especially when changing direction.

Carnivores

Cheetahs are **carnivores** and need to eat as much as 6.5 pounds (3 kilograms) of meat every day. They usually hunt animals such as deer, antelope, and hares, although sometimes they will also catch warthogs and birds. Cheetahs get plenty of water from the food that they eat so they only drink fresh water every few days.

Cheetah jaws

A cheetah has extra large nostrils so that it can breathe in a lot of air when running fast. This leaves less room for its jaws and teeth, which are smaller than those in other big cats.

Cheetah teeth

A cheetah uses its long, pointed teeth to grip its prey firmly. A cheetah slices through its food using its back teeth and then swallows it in large chunks.

After it has killed its prey, a cheetah will drag it away and eat it quickly.

FANTASTIC FACTS

It takes a cheetah about three years to become a fully skilled hunter.
. . . .
Cheetahs hunt and eat prey as large as a young zebra.

Hunting

Cheetahs hunt during the day when larger predators, such as lions, are sleeping. When hunting alone, a cheetah must find prey small enough to bring down and kill by itself. A cheetah hunts by slowly stalking its prey, sometimes for many hours at a time.

Catching prey

When it is close to its prey, a cheetah leaps up and gives chase at high speed for about 20 to 30 seconds. When it is close enough, a cheetah knocks over its prey.

Killing prey

Cheetahs kill small animals, such as gazelles (left), by biting through their necks. Cheetahs **suffocate** large prey by clamping their jaws around the animal's neck.

FANTASTIC FACTS

Cheetahs must slow down when changing direction as they run. This is why prey animals usually zigzag when fleeing.

. . . .

After a long chase, a cheetah may take up to 30 minutes to recover!

When hunting prey, a cheetah creeps closer and closer until it is ready to attack.

Cheetah senses

Cheetahs use their senses of smell, hearing, and sight to find their prey when hunting. The cheetah uses its small, round ears to listen out for sounds. A cheetah's excellent eyesight allows it to see its prey from faraway.

FANTASTIC FACT

Not only can cheetahs see prey that is up to 3 miles (5 kilometers) away, they can also see it in detail.

Listen for danger

All cheetahs listen very carefully for the approach of dangerous predators. From behind, a cheetah's ears look like eyes. A predator may think that the cheetah can see them and not attack.

Looking for prey

A cheetah's eyes face forward, which helps it to tell
how faraway an animal is and how far it has to run.
A cheetah's eyes also have what is known as a "wide
angle of view." This means that when it looks straight
ahead, a cheetah can see to the sides at the same time.

Cheetahs have a large
nose, but their sense of
smell is not as important
as their sense of sight.

Living in a territory

Cheetahs live in an area called a **territory**, where they find their food and water. Territories are not always the same size. Where there is plenty of food, for example, the territory can be small. In desert areas, where food and water are hard to find, a territory can be as big as a large city.

Cheetahs keep watch for intruders in their territory.

Close to their mother

Female cheetahs usually stay in the same area as their mothers and might share parts of her territory.

Cheetah brothers

When cheetah brothers move away from their mother to find their own territory, they usually stay together. Sometimes, they are joined by young males from other families. Young male cheetahs may travel up to 300 miles (480 kilometers) away from their mother and sisters.

FANTASTIC FACT

Males protect their territory by marking boulders and termite mounds with **urine**. They also fight over territory.

Cheetah talk

Cheetahs make many sounds to communicate with each other when resting and hunting. However, cheetahs cannot roar like lions, because the bones in their throat are hard and close together.

FANTASTIC FACT

A cheetah makes a high-pitched chirping that sounds just like a birdcall. Birds hear the chirping and fly down. Then the cheetah catches them!

When two adult cheetahs meet, they greet each other by making a soft churring sound.

Purring and growling

When it is happy and relaxed, a cheetah will purr gently like a pet cat. Unlike a pet cat, however, which can purr continuously, a cheetah only purrs when breathing out.

Calling to cubs

When her cubs have wandered off, a female cheetah makes a distinctive, high-pitched bark as a signal for them to return to her.

Calling to mother

When cubs want to attract their mother, they make a shrill, chirping sound. A cheetah mother can hear her cubs chirping from as faraway as half a mile (800 meters).

Cheetahs and people

In the past, cheetahs were sometimes kept as pets or taken on hunting expeditions. Thankfully, this doesn't happen anymore and cheetahs are left to live free in their natural habitat.

Hunting with a cheetah

Cheetahs were first tamed and used for hunting about 5,000 years ago by the Sumerians, a people who lived in the Middle East. Later, Arab and Indian princes kept cheetahs for hunting. During a hunt, a cheetah would be released from its cage to run and catch prey after the prey had been found by hunting dogs.

Egyptian pharaohs

Records show that the pharaohs of ancient Egypt kept cheetahs as pets. A cheetah was considered to be extremely valuable, and many paintings and statues of cheetahs, such as this one (left) have been discovered in ancient Egyptian sites.

Today, cheetahs are protected in the wild rather than kept as pets.

FANTASTIC FACT

Emperor Akbar the Great of India, who ruled between 1555 and 1600, owned about 1,000 cheetahs. Sadly, only one litter of cubs was born during the many years that he kept cheetahs.

Cheetahs under threat

One hundred years ago, over 100,000 cheetahs could be found living in the wild. Today, there are fewer than 10,000, making the cheetah an **endangered** animal that is at risk of becoming **extinct**.

Loss of habitats

In the past, many cheetahs were hunted for their fur, which was used to make expensive coats. Cheetahs were also killed by farmers, who wanted to protect their **livestock**. Today, the main threat to cheetahs comes from the loss of their habitat.

FANTASTIC FACT

Tourists to national parks bring money to the area, which helps fund the parks.

Losing land

Cheetahs are still under threat, sadly, as more and more of the grasslands where cheetahs live are being used to graze cattle and sheep and to grow crops.

Saving cheetahs

People are making a big effort to save the cheetah. Animals are now being protected in national parks, where hunting and grazing is banned. Instead, tourists are invited to watch cheetahs.

Watching a cheetah is often the highlight of a safari trip in Africa.

Life cycle of a cheetah

A female cheetah is ready to breed when she is about two years old. She gives birth to between three and five cubs. The cubs stay with her for up to 18 months. A cheetah lives for between five and 12 years in the wild but up to 17 years in a zoo.

cub

older cheetah

adult

Glossary

carnivores animals that eat other animals

endangered animals that may become extinct if something is not done to protect them

extinct animals or plants that have died out completely

habitat the place in which an animal or plant lives

litter two or more young animals born together, to one mother

livestock farm animals, such as cows, pigs, and chickens

predators animals that hunt and eat other animals

pregnant describes a female animal that has a baby, or babies, developing inside of her

prey an animal that is hunted by other animals

retracted pulled in, as a cat can pull in its claws

savanna grassland in a hot country

subspecies groups within a species that look slightly different from each other

suffocate to die because breathing is prevented

territory an area in which an animal spends its life and where it finds all of its food and water

urine waste liquid that is passed out of the body

Index

ANIMAL LIVES

CHEETAHS

How fast is a cheetah?

Why do cheetahs have spots?

Where in the world do cheetahs live?

Learn all about the amazing world of cheetahs, and follow their lives from cub to adult.

You'll be an expert in no time!

ISBN 978-1-78171-614-4

9 781781 716144

Dinah Zike's

Big Book of Science

FOR MIDDLE SCHOOL AND HIGH SCHOOL

Read, Write, Research

find similarities and differences
investigative experimentation
compare and contrast
illustrate and label
cause and effect
pros and cons
hypothesize
investigate
measure
explain
inquire
define
prove
graph
map
list
chart
justify
identify
discuss
observe
discover
determine
make tables
draw diagrams
search the web
sequence events
develop a time line
differentiate between
who, what, when, where
what, where, when, why/how